9-12-95
(25)   9-09

37.10/2018

D1482309

	DATE DUE	
MAR 2 7 1996		
MAR 0 5 1996		

Devonshire, Hilary.
    Light / Hilary Devonshire. -- New York : F.
Watts, c1991.

    32 p. : ill. ; w 4-6. -- (Science through
art)

    SUMMARY: Examines the various properties of
light and offers a number of projects
demonstrating these principles.
    ISBN 0-531-14126-8(lib.bdg.) : $11.40
                        58642
                                    OCT '92

    1. Light. 2. Light--Experiments.   I.
Title. II. Series.

9-12-95

50

SCIENCE THROUGH Art

Light

Hilary Devonshire

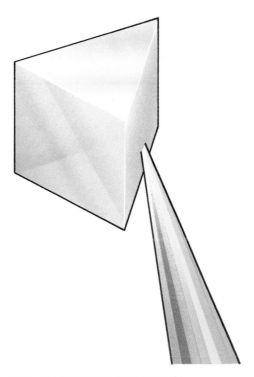

FRANKLIN WATTS
New York/London/Toronto/Sydney

© Franklin Watts 1991

Franklin Watts, Inc.
387 Park Avenue South
New York, NY 10016

Series Editor: Hazel Poole
Editor: Jenny Wood
Design: K and Co
Artwork: Aziz Khan
Photography: Chris Fairclough; Eye Ubiquitous/Dorothy Burrows (p5)
Photographs p21(m), p30(m) reproduced by
kind permission of The Electricity Association
Consultants: Henry Pluckrose, Barbara Taylor,
Lillian Wright

Library of Congress Cataloging-in-Publication Data

Devonshire, Hilary.
    Light / Hilary Devonshire.
        p.   cm. — (Science through art)
    Includes bibliographical references and index.
    Summary: Examines the various properties of light and offers a
number of projects demonstrating these principles.
    ISBN 0-531-14126-8
    1. Light—Juvenile literature.   2. Light—Experiments—Juvenile
literature.   [1. Light.   2. Light—Experiments.   3. Experiments.]
I. Title.   II. Series.
QC360.D48   1991
535—dc20
                                                              91-8401
                                                              CIP AC

Typeset by Lineage, Watford

Printed in the United Kingdom

CONTENTS

EQUIPMENT AND MATERIALS

This book describes activities which use the following:

Adhesives – clear cold water paste (for example, wallpaper paste)

Battery

Bowl (large)

Camera with flash unit

Cardboard (thin, white)

Cardboard boxes

Cardboard tubes (toilet paper roll centers)

Cellophane (assorted colors)

Compass

Cooking oil

Cotton balls

Craft knife

Crayons

Dowel rods

Fabric (assorted scraps)

Felt-tip pens

Flashlight

Flashlight bulb and bulb holder

Graph paper

India ink (black)

Mirrors – concave
– convex
– flat (one large, two small)
– flexible

Paintbrushes

Paints

Paper – white, black and colored
– assorted scraps of shiny, metallic papers
– tissue paper (white and red)

Paper fasteners

Pen

Pencil

Polar grid paper

Ruler (metal)

Scissors

Tape

Toothpick

Water

White glue

Wire

INTRODUCTION

Light is a form of energy. Natural light comes to earth from our nearest star, the sun. All stars give off light energy, but the sun is by far the nearest. Light from the sun travels through space at the incredible speed of 299,260 kilometers (186,000 miles) per second, and takes eight minutes to reach earth. A ray of light from the next nearest star would take over four years!

Light is important to us because, without light, the world would change completely. The light that reaches our eyes allows us to see and make sense of everything around us.

People have discovered ways of making artificial light in order to see when there is no sunlight. At first, fire was used to give light. Later, people burned candles, as well as oil and gas lamps. Today, most of our artificial light is provided by electricity.

By following the investigations in this book, you will learn something about the science of light. At the start of each section there are some scientific ideas to be explored. A scientist looks at ideas and tries to discover if they are always true, and will also investigate to see if they can be *disproved*. You will be working like a scientist. A scientist is curious and wants to find out about the world in which we live. A scientist tests ideas, makes investigations and experiments, and tries to explain what has happened. Your results may be surprising or unexpected, and then you may find that you will need to make a new investigation or test a new idea.

You will also be an artist. You will be using light in the art activities that are included in each section. Through working with light and the various art materials and techniques, you will make discoveries about how light behaves and how light can be used. Your finished pieces of art will be a record of your scientific findings.

LIGHT FOR SEEING THINGS

Light makes it possible for us to see. Dark is the opposite of light. We see some things, such as the sun and stars, because they give off their own light. But most things do not give off their own light. We are able to see these things because light shines on them and then bounces back, or is reflected, into our eyes.

The most important source of light on earth is the sun. Powerful light rays travel from the sun across space to reach the earth. When the sun sets, the moon may provide light to help us see. The moon does not produce any light of its own. It acts like an enormous mirror, reflecting light from the sun.

Light comes from either natural or artificial sources. The sun and stars are sources of natural light. Electric lamps and candles are sources of artificial light. Artificial light is used to provide extra light on earth, especially when the sun has set.

Night turns into day, and day into night, by the rising and setting of the sun each day.

Moonlight is actually light from the sun, reflected off the surface of the moon.

Sometimes we need to make use of artificial light. Artificial light sources include electric lamps and candles.

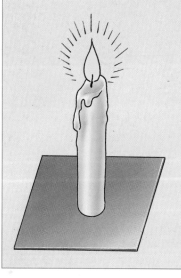

Look outside on a dark night. There may be lights in houses, streetlights, moonlight, etc. What lights can you see?

How many things can light up your home? How many of them are lit up by electricity? If you had no electricity indoors, what might be used to give light?

A picture in a tube

You will need: black paper, scissors, glue, tape, white tissue paper, a cardboard tube (such as a toilet paper roll).

1. Cut a silhouette shape from the black paper. Glue the shape onto a circle of white tissue paper slightly larger in size than the opening of the cardboard tube.

2. Tape the tissue paper circle over the tube opening so that you can see the silhouette when you look through the tube.

3. Cut out a circle of black paper, large enough to fit over the tissue paper circle. Attach a tab to the black paper circle. Place this circle over the tissue paper circle and glue the tab to the side of the tube.

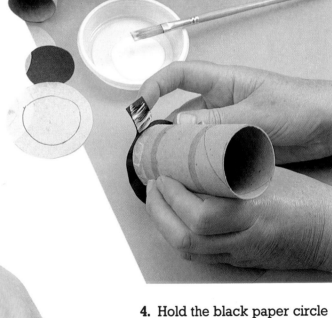

4. Hold the black paper circle tightly over the end of the tube and look through the tube once more. You will not be able to see the silhouette this time. The tube is dark.

5. Ask a friend if they can see anything. Then lift the black circle away. A surprise picture!

Day and night

You will need: thin white cardboard, a pencil, a compass, paints, paintbrushes, a paper fastener.

1. Draw a pencil line across the center of a piece of cardboard. Make a dot one half inch below the center of the line. Using a compass, and with the dot as the center, draw a semicircle above the line with a radius equal to the distance from the dot to the bottom of the cardboard…

… On the second piece of cardboard, draw a circle with the same radius as that used on the first piece of cardboard. Draw a second, larger circle outside the first, its radius one half inch wider.

2. Paint a daytime sky on one half of the inner circle, and a nighttime sky on the other half. Cut out your circle, around the outer edge.

3. Paint a scene around the semicircle on the first piece of cardboard, then cut away the semicircular space.

4. Push the paper fastener through the dot below the line, then through the center of the circle. Open out the fastener.

5. Rotate the cardboard circle inside the scene. Here it is day...

... and here it is night!

Artificial light

You will need: a battery, wire,
flashlight, bulb holder.

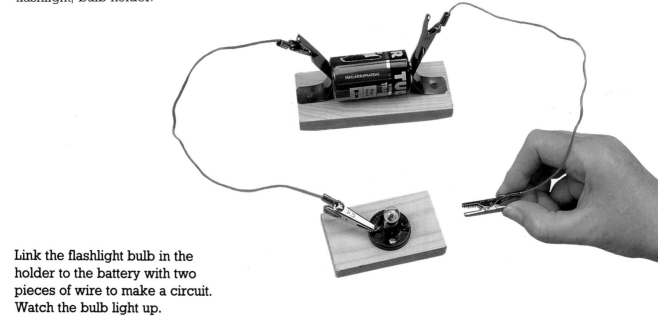

Link the flashlight bulb in the
holder to the battery with two
pieces of wire to make a circuit.
Watch the bulb light up.

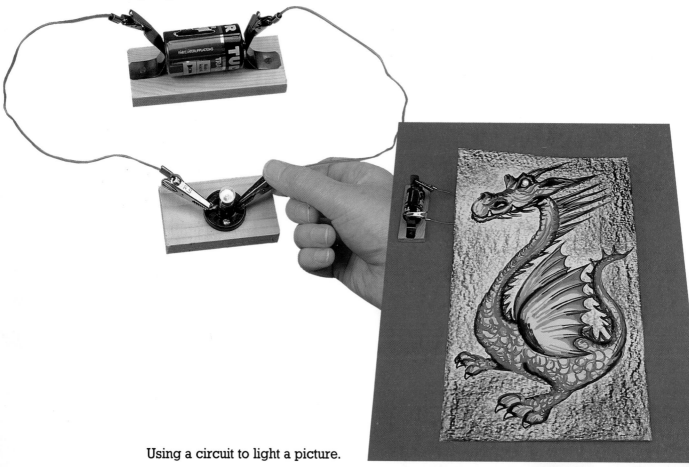

Using a circuit to light a picture.

LIGHT AND SHADOWS

Light travels in straight lines. When light shines on an object, a dark image called a shadow forms behind it. A shadow occurs because rays of light travel in straight lines and cannot bend around the object to light up the shadow area.

The position and size of the light shining on an object make a difference to the size and sharpness of the object's shadow.

A shadow is created behind an object because light rays cannot go around it.

Look at your shadow on a sunny day. Early in the day, the sun will cast long shadows. At midday, the sun has moved higher in the sky and therefore casts shorter shadows. Stand on the same spot at different times of the day and notice how your shadow changes.

Shadow pictures

You will need: a pencil, felt-tip pens or crayons, thin cardboard, a craft knife, a metal ruler, a flashlight.

1. Draw a picture on a piece of cardboard. Using the craft knife, cut along the top and side edges of the picture. Do *not* cut along the bottom edge. Instead, make a fold along this edge so that the picture will stand up.

2. Stand your picture in front of a white background. Shine the flashlight onto the front of your picture. Look behind your picture. What do you notice?

Try moving your picture farther away from the background. Watch the shadows to see what happens.

A moving figure

You will need: a pencil, felt-tip pens or crayons, thin cardboard, scissors, a flashlight, paper fasteners, tape, dowel rods, red cellophane (or red tissue paper).

1. Draw the body of your figure on a piece of cardboard. Draw the two arms and the two legs separately. Cut out the pieces.

2. Attach the arms and legs to the figure's body, using the paper fasteners.

3. Tape a dowel rod to the back of the figure. Hold the figure in front of a white background, shine a flashlight onto it, and make its shadow dance.

4. What happens to the color of the shadow if you cover the flashlight with red cellophane or red tissue paper? Experiment further using green and blue cellophane.

> WARNING! CELLOPHANE IS FLAMMABLE. DO NOT USE IT OVER AN ELECTRIC LIGHT BULB.

5. Can you make a thin shadow of your figure?

OPAQUE, TRANSPARENT AND TRANSLUCENT

Some materials allow light to pass through, so you can see clearly through them. They are called transparent materials.

Some materials, known as translucent materials, also allow light to pass through, but the light is diffused, scattered in different directions. If you look through a translucent object, you will see a blurred image.

Some materials will not let light pass through, so it is impossible to see through them. They are called opaque materials.

Transparent materials allow light to pass through. You can see clearly through a transparent object.

Translucent materials also allow light to pass through, but the light is spread out. If you look through a translucent object, you will see a blurred image.

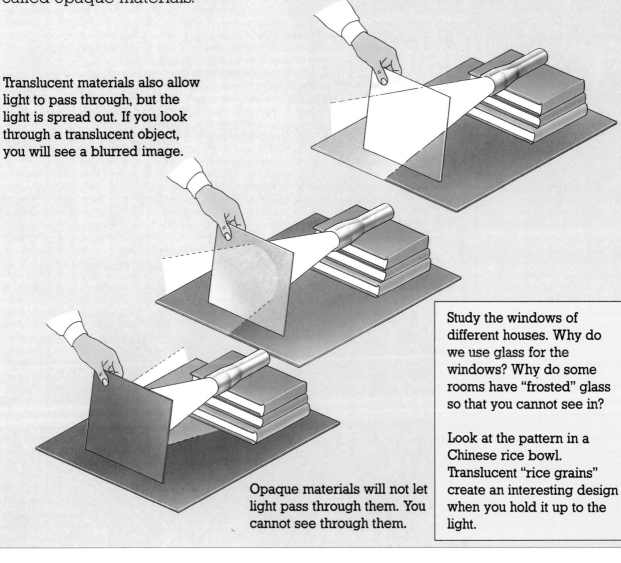

Opaque materials will not let light pass through them. You cannot see through them.

Study the windows of different houses. Why do we use glass for the windows? Why do some rooms have "frosted" glass so that you cannot see in?

Look at the pattern in a Chinese rice bowl. Translucent "rice grains" create an interesting design when you hold it up to the light.

A transparency test

You will need: everyday
objects, paper samples, fabric
samples, flashlight.

1. Look through each object in
turn. How transparent is it?

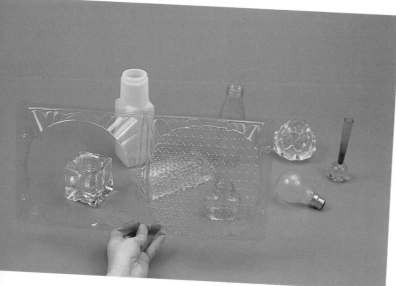

2. Hold each of your paper and
fabric samples in front of the
flashlight. Does the light shine
through?

Screens and Windows

You will need: thin cardboard, white glue, different papers and fabrics, flashlight.

1. Make some screens of thin cardboard. Cut a window in each screen. Fold the screens at the side edges so that they will stand up.

2. Use white glue to stick a piece of paper or fabric over each window. Choose a different material for each, for example, white tissue paper, black construction paper, plastic bubble wrap, paper, thin white fabric.

3. Arrange your screens in a row in front of a white background. Light your screens from the front. Observe the shadows made by the different materials you have used. How transparent are your windows? Notice how the screens themselves make a very dark shadow because they are opaque.

Move your light to one side, then the other. What do you notice?

A cutout design

Use thin cardboard and a craft knife to make a silhouette design. Hang your design in front of a window so that the light can shine through.

A stained glass window

You will need: a pencil, white paper, black India ink, crayons, cooking oil and cotton balls.

1. Draw a window on one of the sheets of white paper, then draw a design within the window. Go over the lines of your design with India ink, and leave to dry. Use the crayons to color in the design.

2. Using a small quantity of cooking oil on a cotton ball, rub this gently over the *back* of your design. The India ink will resist the oil, but the oil will soak into the crayon areas. This will make your design translucent. Leave to dry.

3. Tape your design to a window, and allow the light to shine through. Hold the second sheet of white paper so that the light falls through your design onto the paper.

Stage Lighting

You will need: a cardboard box, some thin cardboard, craft knife, felt-tip pens, a flashlight and colored cellophane.

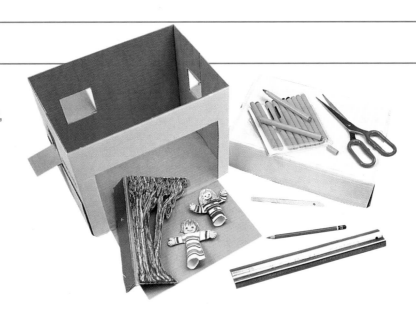

1. Use the cardboard box to make a theater stage. Cut windows which open at the back and side of the stage. Make some standing figures and scenery from the thin cardboard, and color with the felt-tip pens.

2. Light your stage from the back. Have the figures cast any shadows?

3. Now light your stage from the side. Where are the shadows now?

4. Try lighting your stage from the front. You could cover your flashlight with colored cellophane, to use as a spotlight. Ask a friend to hold a second flashlight, with a different color. Observe the color and position of the shadows.

> **WARNING: CELLOPHANE IS FLAMMABLE. DO NOT USE IT OVER AN ELECTRIC LIGHT BULB.**

5. Paint and decorate your theater, and design scenery and figures for a box theater play.

REFLECTED LIGHT

When light falls on a shiny or polished surface, it is reflected. The light doesn't travel through the object, but is bounced back. You can see good reflections in a shiny spoon, a polished table, or the water in a pond or lake if the surface is still.

When light falls on a shiny surface, it bounces back. This is called reflection.

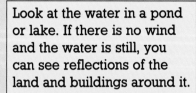

Look at the water in a pond or lake. If there is no wind and the water is still, you can see reflections of the land and buildings around it.

Bicycles and cars have reflectors. At night these will reflect the light from the cars behind. Some road signs are also made of reflective material. How many other examples can you find of reflective materials being used?

A shiny paper collage

1. Make a collection of different types of shiny paper.

2. Cut and arrange the papers to make a picture. Use white glue to mount your picture on cardboard.

3. "Silver boat on a silver sea." Notice how the large amount of reflected light from the shiny, metallic surfaces of the paper pieces makes the overall appearance of the collage very bright.

MIRRORS

Mirrors are specially designed to reflect light. A mirror is usually a flat sheet of glass with a thin layer of shiny metal, such as silver or aluminum behind the glass.

The reflected image of an object as seen in a mirror is identical to the object, but reversed (the opposite way around).

How many different kinds of mirrors can you find in your home? How are they used?

A mirror gives an exact reflection of an object, but in reverse.

Reflected images

You will need: a large flat mirror, paper, colored chalk, pastels, a pen and a ruler.

2a. Fold a piece of paper in half. Open the paper and write your name in chalk along the line of the fold. Fold the paper again so that you get an impression in chalk of your name on the other half of the paper. Write over this reflected image of your name.

1. Sit in front of an ordinary flat mirror and draw a picture of yourself as accurately as you can. If you use chalks or pastels, you can blend the colors with your fingers. Now try to write your first name under your picture, while you look at it in the mirror.

b. Place a mirror along the line of the fold. Look at the reflection of your reflected image. What do you notice?

A reflected design

When you look through a kaleidoscope, you will see a number of reflected images which together create a pattern.

You will need: paper, a pencil, a ruler, felt-tip pens, two small, flat mirrors.

1. On a sheet of paper, draw two lines which cross each other at right angles (90°). Using the felt-tip pens, draw a picture or pattern inside one right-angled section.

2. Stand two mirrors upright along the lines of the section. The mirrors should touch where the lines cross. What do you see?

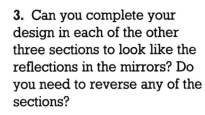

3. Can you complete your design in each of the other three sections to look like the reflections in the mirrors? Do you need to reverse any of the sections?

What happens if you position the two mirrors at different angles?

How many mirrors are used in a kaleidoscope to create the patterns?

"Picture in reflection"

MIRRORS – CONCAVE AND CONVEX

Some mirrors are designed in special ways. Concave mirrors are curved, with the curve bending away from the viewer. They reflect light rays in such a way that the rays come together (converge) at a fixed point and enlarge the image.

Convex mirrors also curve, but this time the curve bends toward the viewer. Convex mirrors collect light from a wide angle and reflect it in a narrow beam. The image is reduced in size.

Concave mirrors curve away from the viewer (that is, like a cave). They enlarge the image.

Convex mirrors curve outward toward the viewer. They reduce the image.

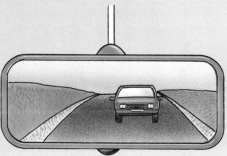

Look at the driver's mirror in a car. Is it concave or convex? Compare this mirror with the wing mirrors. What do you notice?

Flexible Mirrors

A flexible mirror is a shiny sheet of thin reflective metal or plastic which you can bend to make concave or convex.

You will need: some white paper, a pencil and a flexible mirror.

1. Bend your flexible mirror into a concave mirror. Place an object in front of the mirror, and look at its reflection.

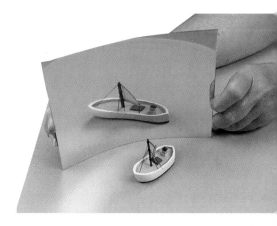

2. Bend your flexible mirror into a convex mirror. Place the same object in front of the mirror and look at its reflection now.

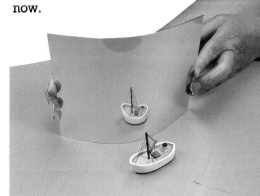

What happens to the reflection if you bend the flexible mirror forward at the top and at the bottom?

Light reflected in a shiny ladle – a convex curve. What will the image be like on the other side?

3. Stand your flexible mirror on a piece of paper and bend it back at both sides so that it becomes a convex mirror once more. Look in the mirror and try to draw a straight line. What happens?

If you draw a curved line, parallel to the bottom edge of the mirror, its reflection in the mirror will appear straight.

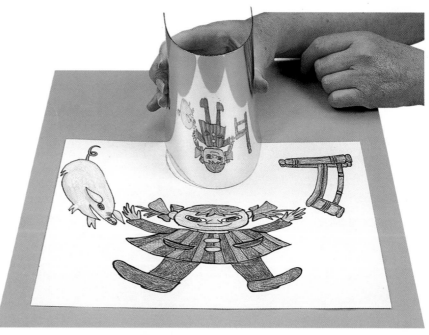

4. You can use this idea to try to draw a curved picture so that when it is reflected in a convex mirror it appears normal.

Polar grid

You will need: graph paper, a
sheet of polar grid paper, a
ruler, a pencil, a flexible mirror.

1. Draw a simple house on
graph paper noting the
coordinates.

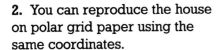

2. You can reproduce the house
on polar grid paper using the
same coordinates.

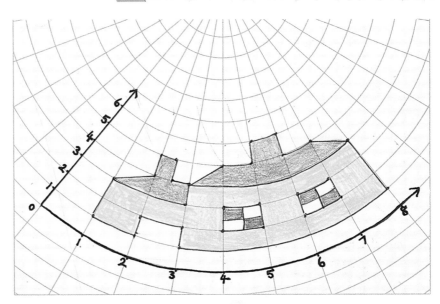

3. Place your convex mirror on
a curved line above the house.
What do you notice about the
image in the mirror?

4. Experiment with your
mirror, and with other

Do you think that polar grid
paper could help you with
your curved picture on
page 24?

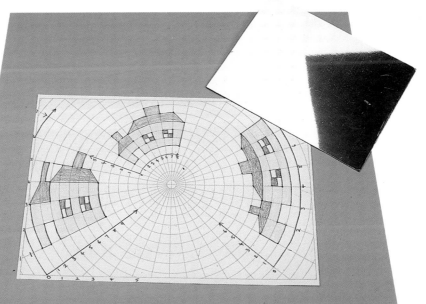

BENDING LIGHT

If a beam of light is bent, it is refracted. It breaks up into the colors of the spectrum – red, orange, yellow, green, blue, indigo and violet. We can see the colors of the spectrum if light passes through a specially cut piece of class called a prism. Inside the prism, the light is bent, or refracted. When it emerges from the other side, the seven separate colors of the spectrum can be seen clearly.

Light is made up of seven colors, which together form a band of colors known as the spectrum.

When a beam of light passes through a glass prism, it is possible to see the seven individual colors of the spectrum. The light is bent, or "refracted," inside the prism.

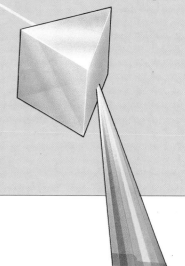

Raindrops act like tiny prisms. When the sun shines during a fall of rain, the raindrops refract the light to form a rainbow.

Have you seen a rainbow in the sky? What color is at its outer edge?

Look for the colors of a spectrum.

The spectrum

You will need: a flat mirror, a flashlight and a large bowl of water.

1. You can make a spectrum by shining a flashlight onto a mirror held at an angle under water. The light bends as it enters the water and is refracted.

Red, green and blue are the main colors in light. They are known as the primary light colors. Other colors can be made by mixing these colors.

A color wheel

You will need: thin cardboard, a compass, a pencil, paints, paintbrushes, white glue and a toothpick.

1. Draw and cut out two circles of cardboard. Divide one circle into four sections, and color the sections red and green alternately.

2. Glue the two circles together to make your wheel thicker and firmer. Push the toothpick through the center and glue it in position. Leave to dry. Spin the wheel. What color do you see?

3. What colors are made from a red and blue wheel, a blue and green wheel, and a red, blue and green wheel?

Make a color wheel using all the colors of the spectrum. What happens to the colors when you spin this wheel?

OPTICAL ILLUSION

At the beginning of this book, we discovered that without light we cannot see. The study of light and the way the eye detects light is called optics.

Sometimes your eyes may appear to see something that is not really there. This is called an optical illusion. In fact, your eyes do see correctly, but your brain interprets the messages from your eyes incorrectly.

Do you see two faces or a candlestick? This is a well-known example of an optical illusion.

Afterimages

You will need: two sheets of white paper and a red felt-tip pen.

1. Draw a ¾ in square on the first sheet of white paper. Color it with the red felt-tip pen. Look at it steadily while you count slowly to 40, then look away and straight at the second sheet of white paper. What do you notice?

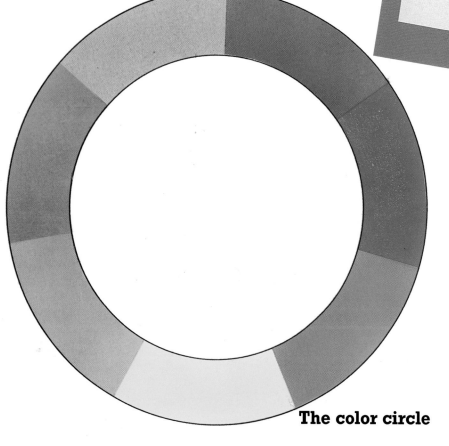

The colored image that you see is called the afterimage. Its color is on the opposite side of the color circle from the original color. The colors are *complementary.* At the back of your eyes are special cells which respond to red, green and blue light. If you stare at a red square, the cells that respond to red light get tired. So when you look away, and at a white sheet of paper, the red cells stop working and have a rest. Only the green and blue cells are working, so you see a green blue square.

The color circle

2. Try again using a green or blue colored square. Then experiment with other shapes (triangle, circle, hexagon).

You will need: a camera flash unit.

1. Take a camera flash unit into a dark room. Concentrate your eyes on a section of the room close to you, then fire the flash gun. At first, everything will appear dark. Slowly, an afterimage of the part of the room at which you were looking will appear very clearly.

Op art

Op art is fun. In op art, pictures often appear to move. Complementary colors such as black and white, or red and green, are used to create the optical illusion of movement.

1. Make your own op art picture. A cardboard pattern with a curved edge will help you create a regular pattern.

The bright flash of light from a flash gun overstimulates the light-sensitive cells in your eyes. They keep sending messages to your brain even when the light is no longer there, so you think you can still "see" the light.

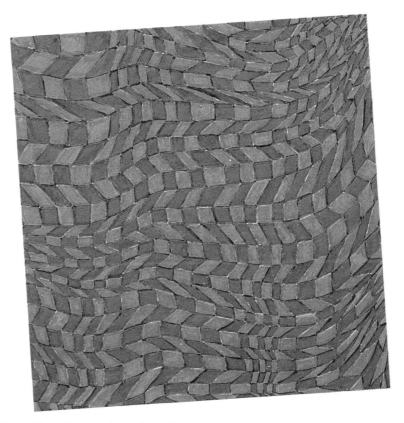

A dazzling design in red and green.

FURTHER IDEAS

A shadow puppet

You can use the moving figure (p12) as a shadow puppet. Attach a rod to the back of the puppet. Make a screen from white sheeting or thin linen. Hold the puppet against the screen and shine a light from behind. The audience will see a shadow image on the screen.

A pink elephant

Paint a green elephant on a sheet of white paper. Stare at the elephant while you count to 40. Look away at a piece of white paper or a white wall. You will "see" a pink elephant!

Collage

Make a picture which incorporates a piece of reflective paper. In this painting, silver paper has been used for the mirror in the living room.

An illustrated dictionary

Make an illustrated dictionary of words which have links with light.

Here are some examples:
lighthouse	flashlight
lightning	headlight
light-year	sunlight

A photographic study

Use a camera to take photographs of how light is used in our world. You can begin by using the ideas mentioned in each section of this book.

GLOSSARY

Color circle
A circle of the colors of the spectrum.

Complementary colors
These pairs of colors appear on opposite sides of the color circle.

Concave mirror
A mirror that bends forward at the edges in a regular curve. It enlarges the image.

Convex mirror
A mirror that bends back at the edges in a regular curve. It reduces the image.

Dark
Opposite of light. There is no light.

Illuminate
To light up.

Image
A copy of an object in reflection, shadows or pictures.

Light
Opposite of dark. We need light to see. Light comes naturally from the sun. It travels in space at the speed of 186,000 miles in one second.

Luminous
Giving light; shining or bright. For example, luminous paint.

Mirror
A device for reflecting light. A flat mirror produces a reflected image of an object that is identical to the object, but the opposite way around.

Opaque
Not transparent, for example, does not allow light to pass through.

Optical illusion
A mismatch between what is seen by the eye and what is interpreted by the brain.

Optics
The study of light and the way the eye detects light.

Reflection
The bouncing back of light from a polished surface or mirror to give an image of the object.

Refraction
Changing the direction of a beam of light and making it appear to bend. The refraction of white (ordinary) light can produce a spectrum of the seven colors which make up white light.

Shadow
A dark image of an object caused by light passing by, but not through, the object.

Silhouette
The outline of a person or object. A silhouette is often a black image on a white background.

Spectrum
A colored band of seven colors: red, orange, yellow, green, blue, indigo and violet. It is caused by the refraction of light. You can see the spectrum in a rainbow, or when light passes through a glass prism.

Translucent
Some light passes through translucent materials but it is diffused (scattered). If you look through a translucent object, you will see a blurred image.

Transparent
Allows light to pass through. You can see clearly through transparent materials.